50 Family-Friendly Dinner Recipes for Home

By: Kelly Johnson

Table of Contents

- Spaghetti Bolognese
- Chicken Alfredo Pasta
- Beef Tacos
- Vegetable Stir-Fry
- Margherita Pizza
- Chicken Parmesan
- BBQ Chicken Drumsticks
- Shrimp Fried Rice
- Meatball Subs
- Grilled Cheese Sandwiches
- Baked Ziti
- Chicken Teriyaki
- Sloppy Joes
- Chicken Quesadillas
- Fish Tacos
- Beef and Broccoli
- Veggie Lasagna
- Chicken Enchiladas
- Turkey Burgers
- Lemon Garlic Roast Chicken
- Teriyaki Salmon
- Chili Con Carne
- Chicken Caesar Salad
- Pulled Pork Sandwiches
- Spicy Chickpea Curry
- Hawaiian Pizza
- Turkey Meatball Soup
- Creamy Chicken and Rice Casserole
- Caprese Chicken
- Tofu Stir-Fry
- Baked Chicken Nuggets
- Vegetable Pizza
- Chicken and Broccoli Alfredo
- Sweet Potato Black Bean Quesadillas
- One-Pan Baked Zucchini and Tomato Chicken

- Creamy Tomato Basil Pasta
- Buffalo Chicken Wraps
- Lemon Herb Grilled Chicken
- Teriyaki Veggie Bowl
- Chicken and Rice Burrito Bowls
- Beef and Mushroom Stroganoff
- Pesto Pasta with Cherry Tomatoes
- Veggie-loaded Spaghetti Carbonara
- Oven-Baked BBQ Chicken
- Lemon Garlic Shrimp Pasta
- Broccoli Cheddar Stuffed Potatoes
- Turkey and Veggie Skillet
- Chicken Fajita Bowls
- Spinach and Feta Stuffed Chicken Breast
- Mediterranean Quinoa Salad

Spaghetti Bolognese

Ingredients:

- 1 pound (450g) ground beef or ground plant-based meat substitute
- 1 tablespoon olive oil
- 1 onion, finely chopped
- 2 carrots, grated
- 2 celery stalks, finely chopped
- 3 cloves garlic, minced
- 1 can (28 ounces) crushed tomatoes
- 1/2 cup red wine (optional)
- 1 teaspoon dried oregano
- 1 teaspoon dried basil
- 1/2 teaspoon dried thyme
- 1 bay leaf
- Salt and pepper, to taste
- 1/2 cup whole milk or non-dairy milk
- 1 pound (450g) spaghetti
- Grated Parmesan cheese or nutritional yeast (optional, for serving)
- Fresh basil or parsley, chopped (for garnish)

Instructions:

In a large skillet or pot, heat the olive oil over medium heat. Add the ground beef (or plant-based meat substitute) and cook until browned, breaking it up with a spoon as it cooks.

Add the chopped onion, grated carrots, chopped celery, and minced garlic to the skillet. Cook for about 5 minutes or until the vegetables are softened.

Pour in the crushed tomatoes and red wine (if using). Stir in the dried oregano, basil, thyme, bay leaf, salt, and pepper.

Bring the mixture to a simmer, then reduce the heat to low and let it cook for at least 30 minutes to allow the flavors to meld. Stir occasionally.

While the sauce is simmering, cook the spaghetti according to the package instructions. Drain and set aside.

After the sauce has simmered, stir in the milk and let it cook for an additional 5-10 minutes.

Taste and adjust the seasoning as needed. Remove the bay leaf.

Serve the Bolognese sauce over the cooked spaghetti.
Optionally, top with grated Parmesan cheese or nutritional yeast and garnish with fresh basil or parsley.
Enjoy this classic and hearty Spaghetti Bolognese!

Chicken Alfredo Pasta

Ingredients:

- 8 ounces (225g) fettuccine pasta
- 2 tablespoons unsalted butter
- 1 pound (450g) boneless, skinless chicken breasts, cut into bite-sized pieces
- Salt and pepper, to taste
- 2 cloves garlic, minced
- 1 cup heavy cream
- 1 cup grated Parmesan cheese
- 1/2 cup grated mozzarella cheese
- 1/2 teaspoon garlic powder
- 1/2 teaspoon onion powder
- 1/2 teaspoon dried Italian herbs (optional)
- Fresh parsley, chopped (for garnish)

Instructions:

Cook the fettuccine pasta according to the package instructions. Drain and set aside.
In a large skillet, melt the butter over medium heat.
Season the chicken pieces with salt and pepper. Add them to the skillet and cook until browned and cooked through.
Add the minced garlic to the skillet and cook for about 1 minute until fragrant.
Pour in the heavy cream, Parmesan cheese, mozzarella cheese, garlic powder, onion powder, and dried Italian herbs (if using). Stir continuously until the cheese is melted and the sauce is smooth.
Reduce the heat to low and let the sauce simmer for 2-3 minutes until it thickens slightly.
Taste the sauce and adjust the seasoning as needed.
Add the cooked fettuccine pasta to the skillet, tossing to coat the pasta evenly with the Alfredo sauce.
Cook for an additional 2-3 minutes until the pasta is heated through.
Garnish with chopped fresh parsley.
Serve the Chicken Alfredo Pasta immediately, and enjoy this creamy and indulgent dish!

Beef Tacos

Ingredients:

For the Beef Filling:

- 1 pound (450g) ground beef
- 1 tablespoon olive oil
- 1 onion, finely chopped
- 2 cloves garlic, minced
- 1 packet taco seasoning (or use homemade seasoning)
- 1/2 cup water

For Serving:

- 8 small flour or corn tortillas
- Shredded lettuce
- Diced tomatoes
- Shredded cheese (cheddar or Mexican blend)
- Sour cream or Greek yogurt
- Salsa
- Fresh cilantro, chopped
- Lime wedges

Instructions:

In a large skillet, heat olive oil over medium heat.
Add chopped onions and minced garlic to the skillet. Sauté until the onions are translucent.
Add ground beef to the skillet and cook until browned, breaking it up with a spoon as it cooks.
Drain any excess fat from the beef.
Sprinkle the taco seasoning over the beef and add 1/2 cup of water. Stir well to combine.
Simmer the beef mixture over medium-low heat for 5-7 minutes, allowing the flavors to meld and the liquid to reduce. Adjust seasoning to taste.
While the beef is simmering, warm the tortillas according to package instructions.
Assemble the tacos by spooning the beef mixture onto each tortilla.

Top with shredded lettuce, diced tomatoes, shredded cheese, a dollop of sour cream or Greek yogurt, salsa, and chopped cilantro.

Squeeze a lime wedge over each taco before serving.

Serve the beef tacos immediately, and enjoy the delicious and customizable flavors!

Vegetable Stir-Fry

Ingredients:

For the Stir-Fry Sauce:

- 1/4 cup soy sauce (or tamari for gluten-free)
- 2 tablespoons rice vinegar
- 1 tablespoon sesame oil
- 1 tablespoon maple syrup or agave nectar
- 1 teaspoon cornstarch

For the Vegetable Stir-Fry:

- 2 tablespoons vegetable oil
- 1 bell pepper, thinly sliced
- 1 carrot, julienned
- 1 zucchini, sliced
- 1 broccoli crown, cut into florets
- 1 cup snap peas, trimmed
- 3 green onions, sliced
- 2 cloves garlic, minced
- 1 tablespoon fresh ginger, grated
- Cooked rice or noodles, for serving
- Sesame seeds and chopped cilantro, for garnish (optional)

Instructions:

In a small bowl, whisk together the soy sauce, rice vinegar, sesame oil, maple syrup (or agave nectar), and cornstarch. Set aside.
Heat vegetable oil in a large wok or skillet over medium-high heat.
Add the sliced bell pepper, julienned carrot, sliced zucchini, broccoli florets, and snap peas to the wok. Stir-fry for 3-5 minutes or until the vegetables are crisp-tender.
Add the sliced green onions, minced garlic, and grated ginger to the wok. Stir-fry for an additional 1-2 minutes until fragrant.

Pour the stir-fry sauce over the vegetables. Toss everything to coat evenly and cook for an additional 2-3 minutes until the sauce thickens.
Taste and adjust the seasoning if needed.
Serve the vegetable stir-fry over cooked rice or noodles.
Garnish with sesame seeds and chopped cilantro if desired.
Enjoy this flavorful and colorful vegetable stir-fry as a quick and nutritious meal!

Margherita Pizza

Ingredients:

For the Pizza Dough:

- 1 pound (about 4 cups) pizza dough (store-bought or homemade)
- Flour, for dusting

For the Margherita Pizza:

- 1/2 cup pizza sauce
- 8 ounces fresh mozzarella cheese, sliced
- 2 large tomatoes, sliced
- Fresh basil leaves
- Olive oil, for drizzling
- Salt and pepper, to taste

Instructions:

Preheat your oven to the highest temperature it can reach (usually around 475-500°F or 245-260°C). If you have a pizza stone, place it in the oven to heat.
On a floured surface, roll out the pizza dough to your desired thickness.
If using a pizza stone, transfer the rolled-out dough to a pizza peel or an inverted baking sheet dusted with flour or cornmeal.
Spread pizza sauce evenly over the dough, leaving a small border around the edges.
Arrange slices of fresh mozzarella and tomato evenly on top of the sauce.
Season the pizza with salt and pepper to taste.
If using a pizza stone, carefully transfer the pizza to the preheated stone in the oven. If not using a stone, place the pizza directly on a baking sheet.
Bake in the preheated oven for about 10-12 minutes or until the crust is golden and the cheese is bubbly and slightly browned.
Once out of the oven, scatter fresh basil leaves over the hot pizza.
Drizzle the Margherita pizza with olive oil.
Slice and serve immediately.
Enjoy the classic simplicity and deliciousness of Margherita Pizza!

Chicken Parmesan

Ingredients:

For the Chicken:

- 4 boneless, skinless chicken breasts
- Salt and pepper, to taste
- 1 cup all-purpose flour
- 2 large eggs, beaten
- 1 cup breadcrumbs (plain or seasoned)
- 1/2 cup grated Parmesan cheese
- 2 tablespoons olive oil

For the Assembly:

- 2 cups marinara sauce
- 1 cup shredded mozzarella cheese
- 1/4 cup grated Parmesan cheese
- Fresh basil or parsley, chopped (for garnish)
- Cooked pasta or spaghetti (optional, for serving)

Instructions:

Preheat the oven to 400°F (200°C).
Season the chicken breasts with salt and pepper.
Set up a breading station with three shallow bowls: one with flour, one with beaten eggs, and one with a mixture of breadcrumbs and grated Parmesan.
Dredge each chicken breast in the flour, shaking off any excess.
Dip the chicken in the beaten eggs, allowing any excess to drip off.
Press the chicken into the breadcrumb and Parmesan mixture, coating both sides thoroughly.
Heat olive oil in a large oven-safe skillet over medium-high heat.
Add the breaded chicken breasts to the skillet and cook for 3-4 minutes per side or until golden brown.
Spoon marinara sauce over each chicken breast, followed by a sprinkle of shredded mozzarella and grated Parmesan.

Transfer the skillet to the preheated oven and bake for 20-25 minutes or until the chicken is cooked through and the cheese is melted and bubbly.

If desired, broil for an additional 1-2 minutes to achieve a golden-brown crust on the cheese.

Remove from the oven and let it rest for a few minutes.

Garnish with chopped fresh basil or parsley.

Serve the Chicken Parmesan over cooked pasta or spaghetti if desired.

Enjoy this classic and comforting Chicken Parmesan!

BBQ Chicken Drumsticks

Ingredients:

- 2 pounds (about 10-12) chicken drumsticks
- Salt and pepper, to taste
- 1 teaspoon garlic powder
- 1 teaspoon onion powder
- 1 teaspoon smoked paprika
- 1/2 teaspoon cayenne pepper (optional, for heat)
- 1 cup barbecue sauce (store-bought or homemade)
- 2 tablespoons olive oil
- Fresh parsley, chopped (for garnish, optional)
- Lemon wedges (for serving)

Instructions:

Preheat the oven to 425°F (220°C).
Pat the chicken drumsticks dry with paper towels. Season them with salt, pepper, garlic powder, onion powder, smoked paprika, and cayenne pepper (if using). Rub the seasoning evenly over the drumsticks.
In a bowl, mix together barbecue sauce and olive oil.
Place the drumsticks in a large resealable plastic bag or a bowl. Pour half of the barbecue sauce mixture over the chicken, reserving the other half for later. Seal the bag or cover the bowl and marinate the chicken in the refrigerator for at least 30 minutes, or ideally, overnight.
Line a baking sheet with aluminum foil and place a wire rack on top. Arrange the marinated chicken drumsticks on the rack.
Bake in the preheated oven for 30-40 minutes or until the internal temperature reaches 165°F (74°C) and the chicken is golden brown, turning them halfway through and basting with the remaining barbecue sauce mixture.
If desired, broil for an additional 2-3 minutes to crisp up the skin.
Remove the drumsticks from the oven and let them rest for a few minutes.
Garnish with chopped fresh parsley, if using.
Serve the BBQ Chicken Drumsticks with lemon wedges for squeezing over the top.
Enjoy these flavorful and sticky-sweet BBQ chicken drumsticks as a tasty meal or appetizer!

Shrimp Fried Rice

Ingredients:

- 2 cups cooked white rice (preferably cold and day-old)
- 1 pound (about 450g) large shrimp, peeled and deveined
- 2 tablespoons soy sauce
- 1 tablespoon oyster sauce
- 1 teaspoon sesame oil
- 1 tablespoon vegetable oil
- 3 eggs, lightly beaten
- 1 cup frozen peas and carrots, thawed
- 4 green onions, thinly sliced
- 3 cloves garlic, minced
- 1 teaspoon fresh ginger, grated
- Salt and pepper, to taste

Instructions:

In a bowl, marinate the shrimp with soy sauce, oyster sauce, and sesame oil. Set aside for 10-15 minutes.

Heat vegetable oil in a large skillet or wok over medium-high heat.

Add the marinated shrimp to the skillet and cook for 2-3 minutes per side or until they turn pink and opaque. Remove the shrimp from the skillet and set aside.

In the same skillet, add a bit more oil if needed. Pour in the beaten eggs and scramble them until just set. Remove the scrambled eggs from the skillet and set aside.

Add a bit more oil to the skillet if necessary. Sauté the garlic and ginger until fragrant.

Add the thawed peas and carrots to the skillet and stir-fry for 2-3 minutes.

Add the cold, day-old rice to the skillet. Break up any clumps and stir-fry for 3-5 minutes or until the rice is heated through and starts to turn golden.

Stir in the cooked shrimp, scrambled eggs, and sliced green onions.

Season the shrimp fried rice with salt and pepper to taste. Continue to stir-fry for an additional 2-3 minutes until everything is well combined and heated through.

Serve the shrimp fried rice hot, and enjoy this delicious and quick meal!

Meatball Subs

Ingredients:

For the Meatballs:

- 1 pound (about 450g) ground beef or a mix of ground beef and pork
- 1/2 cup breadcrumbs
- 1/4 cup grated Parmesan cheese
- 1/4 cup fresh parsley, chopped
- 1 teaspoon garlic powder
- 1 teaspoon onion powder
- 1/2 teaspoon dried oregano
- 1/2 teaspoon dried basil
- Salt and pepper, to taste
- 1 large egg
- Olive oil, for cooking

For the Marinara Sauce:

- 2 cups marinara sauce (store-bought or homemade)

For Assembling Subs:

- Hoagie or sub rolls
- Mozzarella cheese, shredded
- Fresh parsley, chopped (for garnish)

Instructions:

For the Meatballs:

> Preheat the oven to 375°F (190°C).
> In a large mixing bowl, combine the ground beef, breadcrumbs, grated Parmesan, chopped parsley, garlic powder, onion powder, dried oregano, dried basil, salt, pepper, and the egg. Mix until well combined.
> Shape the mixture into meatballs, about 1 to 1.5 inches in diameter.

Heat olive oil in a skillet over medium-high heat. Brown the meatballs on all sides, working in batches if necessary.

Transfer the browned meatballs to a baking sheet and bake in the preheated oven for about 15-20 minutes or until cooked through.

For the Marinara Sauce:

In a saucepan, heat the marinara sauce over medium heat until heated through.

For Assembling Subs:

Slice the hoagie or sub rolls lengthwise, leaving one side connected.

Place a layer of shredded mozzarella on one side of each roll.

Spoon a portion of the marinara sauce over the cheese.

Arrange the meatballs on top of the sauce.

Sprinkle additional mozzarella over the meatballs.

Broil the meatball subs in the oven for 2-3 minutes or until the cheese is melted and bubbly.

Remove from the oven and garnish with chopped fresh parsley.

Close the subs and serve them hot.

Enjoy these hearty and flavorful Meatball Subs!

Grilled Cheese Sandwiches

Ingredients:

- 8 slices of bread (white, whole wheat, or your choice)
- Butter or margarine, softened
- 8 slices of cheese (cheddar, Swiss, American, or your favorite)
- Optional additions: sliced tomatoes, cooked bacon, caramelized onions, or ham

Instructions:

Heat a skillet or griddle over medium heat.
Spread a thin layer of softened butter on one side of each slice of bread.
Place the bread slices, buttered side down, on a clean surface.
Add a slice of cheese to the unbuttered side of half of the bread slices.
If desired, add any optional additions like sliced tomatoes, cooked bacon, caramelized onions, or ham on top of the cheese.
Top each sandwich with another slice of bread, buttered side facing out.
Place the sandwiches on the heated skillet or griddle.
Cook for 3-4 minutes on each side or until the bread is golden brown and the cheese is melted.
Press the sandwiches down with a spatula while cooking to ensure even melting.
Once both sides are golden brown and the cheese is melted, remove the grilled cheese sandwiches from the skillet.
Allow the sandwiches to cool for a minute before slicing them diagonally.
Serve the grilled cheese sandwiches warm, and enjoy the gooey goodness!

Feel free to get creative with your grilled cheese by experimenting with different breads, cheeses, and additional ingredients.

Baked Ziti

Ingredients:

- 1 pound (about 450g) ziti pasta
- 1 tablespoon olive oil
- 1 onion, finely chopped
- 2 cloves garlic, minced
- 1 pound (about 450g) ground beef or Italian sausage
- 1 can (28 ounces) crushed tomatoes
- 1 teaspoon dried oregano
- 1 teaspoon dried basil
- Salt and pepper, to taste
- 2 cups ricotta cheese
- 2 cups shredded mozzarella cheese
- 1/2 cup grated Parmesan cheese
- 1/4 cup fresh parsley, chopped (optional)

Instructions:

Preheat the oven to 375°F (190°C).
Cook the ziti pasta according to package instructions until al dente. Drain and set aside.
In a large skillet, heat olive oil over medium heat. Add chopped onions and garlic, and sauté until softened.
Add the ground beef or Italian sausage to the skillet. Cook until browned, breaking it up with a spoon as it cooks.
Pour in the crushed tomatoes and add dried oregano, dried basil, salt, and pepper. Stir well and let the sauce simmer for 15-20 minutes, allowing the flavors to meld.
In a large mixing bowl, combine the cooked ziti with ricotta cheese, half of the shredded mozzarella, half of the grated Parmesan, and chopped parsley if using. Mix well.
In a greased baking dish, layer half of the ziti mixture. Top with half of the meat sauce.
Repeat the layers with the remaining ziti mixture and meat sauce.
Sprinkle the remaining mozzarella and Parmesan cheese over the top.

Cover the baking dish with aluminum foil and bake in the preheated oven for 25-30 minutes.

Remove the foil and bake for an additional 10-15 minutes or until the cheese is melted and bubbly, and the edges are golden brown.

Remove from the oven and let it rest for a few minutes before serving.

Garnish with additional fresh parsley if desired.

Serve the baked ziti hot and enjoy this comforting and cheesy dish!

Chicken Teriyaki

Ingredients:

- 4 boneless, skinless chicken breasts
- Salt and pepper, to taste
- 1/2 cup soy sauce
- 1/4 cup mirin (sweet rice wine)
- 2 tablespoons sake or dry white wine
- 2 tablespoons brown sugar
- 1 tablespoon honey
- 1 tablespoon sesame oil
- 2 cloves garlic, minced
- 1 tablespoon fresh ginger, grated
- 2 green onions, sliced (for garnish)
- Sesame seeds (for garnish)
- Cooked rice, for serving

Instructions:

Season the chicken breasts with salt and pepper.
In a bowl, whisk together soy sauce, mirin, sake (or white wine), brown sugar, honey, sesame oil, minced garlic, and grated ginger to make the teriyaki sauce.
Heat a skillet or grill pan over medium-high heat.
Cook the chicken breasts for 6-8 minutes per side or until fully cooked, basting with some teriyaki sauce during cooking.
In the last few minutes of cooking, brush the chicken with additional teriyaki sauce to glaze.
Once the chicken is cooked through and has a nice glaze, remove it from the skillet and let it rest for a few minutes.
Slice the chicken into strips.
Serve the sliced chicken over cooked rice.
Drizzle extra teriyaki sauce over the chicken.
Garnish with sliced green onions and sesame seeds.
Serve the Chicken Teriyaki hot and enjoy this flavorful and savory dish!

Sloppy Joes

Ingredients:

- 1 pound (about 450g) ground beef
- 1 tablespoon olive oil
- 1 onion, finely chopped
- 1 bell pepper, finely chopped
- 2 cloves garlic, minced
- 1/2 cup ketchup
- 1/4 cup tomato paste
- 2 tablespoons brown sugar
- 1 tablespoon Dijon mustard
- 1 tablespoon Worcestershire sauce
- 1 teaspoon chili powder
- 1/2 teaspoon smoked paprika
- Salt and pepper, to taste
- Hamburger buns, for serving

Instructions:

In a large skillet, heat olive oil over medium heat.
Add chopped onions and bell peppers to the skillet. Sauté until the vegetables are softened.
Add minced garlic to the skillet and cook for an additional 1-2 minutes until fragrant.
Push the vegetables to one side of the skillet and add the ground beef to the other side. Cook the beef, breaking it up with a spoon, until browned.
Combine the cooked vegetables with the browned beef in the skillet.
Stir in ketchup, tomato paste, brown sugar, Dijon mustard, Worcestershire sauce, chili powder, smoked paprika, salt, and pepper. Mix everything well.
Reduce the heat to low and let the mixture simmer for 10-15 minutes, allowing the flavors to meld.
Taste and adjust the seasoning if needed.
Serve the Sloppy Joe mixture on hamburger buns.
Enjoy these classic Sloppy Joes with a side of coleslaw or your favorite accompaniments!

Chicken Quesadillas

Ingredients:

- 2 cups cooked chicken, shredded or diced
- 1 cup shredded cheddar cheese
- 1 cup shredded Monterey Jack cheese
- 1 bell pepper, diced
- 1 small onion, diced
- 1/2 cup diced tomatoes
- 1/4 cup chopped fresh cilantro (optional)
- 1 teaspoon ground cumin
- 1 teaspoon chili powder
- 1/2 teaspoon garlic powder
- Salt and pepper, to taste
- 4 large flour tortillas
- Olive oil or cooking spray, for cooking
- Sour cream, guacamole, and salsa for serving

Instructions:

In a large bowl, combine the cooked chicken, shredded cheddar cheese, shredded Monterey Jack cheese, diced bell pepper, diced onion, diced tomatoes, chopped cilantro (if using), ground cumin, chili powder, garlic powder, salt, and pepper. Mix well.
Heat a large skillet or griddle over medium heat.
Place a tortilla on a flat surface and spoon a portion of the chicken and vegetable mixture onto one half of the tortilla.
Fold the tortilla in half, covering the filling.
Brush the outside of the quesadilla with olive oil or lightly spray with cooking spray.
Place the quesadilla on the heated skillet or griddle and cook for 2-3 minutes on each side, or until the tortilla is golden brown and the cheese is melted.
Repeat the process for the remaining tortillas and filling.
Remove the quesadillas from the skillet and let them cool for a minute before slicing into wedges.
Serve the chicken quesadillas with sour cream, guacamole, and salsa on the side.
Enjoy these delicious and cheesy Chicken Quesadillas as a quick and satisfying meal!

Fish Tacos

Ingredients:

For the Fish:

- 1 pound (about 450g) white fish fillets (tilapia, cod, or any firm white fish)
- 1 teaspoon ground cumin
- 1 teaspoon chili powder
- 1/2 teaspoon garlic powder
- 1/2 teaspoon paprika
- Salt and pepper, to taste
- 2 tablespoons olive oil
- Juice of 1 lime

For the Cabbage Slaw:

- 2 cups shredded green cabbage
- 1/2 cup shredded carrots
- 1/4 cup chopped fresh cilantro
- Juice of 1 lime
- 2 tablespoons mayonnaise (or Greek yogurt for a lighter option)
- Salt and pepper, to taste

For Assembling Tacos:

- Corn or flour tortillas
- Avocado slices
- Salsa
- Lime wedges
- Additional cilantro for garnish

Instructions:

Preheat the oven to 375°F (190°C).
In a small bowl, mix together cumin, chili powder, garlic powder, paprika, salt, and pepper.
Place the fish fillets on a baking sheet lined with parchment paper. Drizzle olive oil and lime juice over the fish.
Sprinkle the spice mixture evenly over the fish fillets.

Bake in the preheated oven for 12-15 minutes or until the fish is cooked through and flakes easily with a fork.

While the fish is baking, prepare the cabbage slaw. In a bowl, combine shredded green cabbage, shredded carrots, chopped cilantro, lime juice, mayonnaise (or Greek yogurt), salt, and pepper. Toss until well combined.

Warm the tortillas according to package instructions.

Once the fish is cooked, break it into bite-sized pieces.

Assemble the fish tacos by placing a spoonful of the cabbage slaw on each tortilla.

Top with pieces of baked fish.

Add avocado slices, salsa, and additional cilantro for garnish.

Serve the fish tacos with lime wedges on the side.

Enjoy these flavorful and fresh Fish Tacos!

Beef and Broccoli

Ingredients:

For the Beef Marinade:

- 1 pound (about 450g) flank steak, thinly sliced
- 2 tablespoons soy sauce
- 1 tablespoon oyster sauce
- 1 tablespoon cornstarch
- 1 teaspoon sesame oil
- 1 teaspoon sugar
- 1/2 teaspoon black pepper

For the Sauce:

- 1/4 cup soy sauce
- 2 tablespoons oyster sauce
- 1 tablespoon hoisin sauce
- 1 tablespoon cornstarch
- 1 tablespoon water

For Cooking:

- 2 tablespoons vegetable oil, divided
- 3 cups broccoli florets
- 3 cloves garlic, minced
- 1 teaspoon fresh ginger, grated
- Cooked white or brown rice, for serving
- Sesame seeds and green onions, for garnish (optional)

Instructions:

In a bowl, combine the sliced flank steak with soy sauce, oyster sauce, cornstarch, sesame oil, sugar, and black pepper. Mix well and let it marinate for at least 15-20 minutes.

In a separate bowl, whisk together soy sauce, oyster sauce, hoisin sauce, cornstarch, and water to make the sauce. Set aside.

Heat 1 tablespoon of vegetable oil in a wok or large skillet over high heat.

Add the marinated beef slices and stir-fry for 2-3 minutes or until browned and cooked through. Remove the beef from the wok and set it aside.

In the same wok, add the remaining 1 tablespoon of vegetable oil.

Stir in minced garlic and grated ginger. Sauté for about 30 seconds until fragrant.

Add broccoli florets to the wok and stir-fry for 2-3 minutes or until they are bright green and slightly tender.

Return the cooked beef to the wok with the broccoli.

Pour the sauce over the beef and broccoli. Stir-fry for an additional 2-3 minutes until the sauce thickens and coats the beef and broccoli evenly.

Serve the beef and broccoli over cooked rice.

Garnish with sesame seeds and sliced green onions if desired.

Enjoy this delicious and savory Beef and Broccoli stir-fry!

Veggie Lasagna

Ingredients:

- 9 lasagna noodles, cooked according to package instructions
- 2 tablespoons olive oil
- 1 onion, finely chopped
- 2 cloves garlic, minced
- 1 zucchini, diced
- 1 yellow squash, diced
- 1 bell pepper, diced (any color)
- 1 carrot, grated
- 1 cup sliced mushrooms
- 1 (28 ounces) can crushed tomatoes
- 1 (14 ounces) can diced tomatoes, drained
- 1 teaspoon dried oregano
- 1 teaspoon dried basil
- Salt and pepper, to taste
- 2 cups ricotta cheese
- 2 cups shredded mozzarella cheese
- 1/2 cup grated Parmesan cheese
- 1 large egg
- 1/4 cup fresh basil, chopped (optional)

Instructions:

Preheat the oven to 375°F (190°C).
In a large skillet, heat olive oil over medium heat. Add chopped onions and garlic, and sauté until softened.
Add diced zucchini, yellow squash, bell pepper, grated carrot, and sliced mushrooms to the skillet. Cook for 5-7 minutes or until the vegetables are tender.
Pour in the crushed tomatoes and drained diced tomatoes. Add dried oregano, dried basil, salt, and pepper. Stir well and let the sauce simmer for 10-15 minutes.
In a bowl, mix together ricotta cheese, shredded mozzarella, grated Parmesan, and the egg. Stir in chopped fresh basil if using.
Spread a thin layer of the vegetable-tomato sauce in the bottom of a 9x13-inch baking dish.
Place three cooked lasagna noodles on top of the sauce.

Spread half of the ricotta cheese mixture over the noodles.
Spoon half of the remaining vegetable-tomato sauce over the cheese layer.
Repeat the layers, finishing with a layer of sauce on top.
Sprinkle additional mozzarella and Parmesan cheese on top if desired.
Cover the baking dish with aluminum foil and bake in the preheated oven for 30 minutes.
Remove the foil and bake for an additional 15-20 minutes or until the cheese is melted and bubbly, and the edges are golden brown.
Let the veggie lasagna rest for a few minutes before slicing.
Serve the veggie lasagna hot and enjoy this hearty and flavorful dish!

Chicken Enchiladas

Ingredients:

For the Chicken Filling:

- 2 cups cooked and shredded chicken (rotisserie chicken works well)
- 1 cup black beans, drained and rinsed
- 1 cup corn kernels (fresh, frozen, or canned)
- 1 cup diced bell peppers (any color)
- 1 cup diced onions
- 1 teaspoon ground cumin
- 1 teaspoon chili powder
- Salt and pepper, to taste
- 2 cups shredded Mexican blend cheese

For the Enchilada Sauce:

- 2 tablespoons olive oil
- 2 tablespoons all-purpose flour
- 1 tablespoon chili powder
- 1 teaspoon ground cumin
- 1/2 teaspoon garlic powder
- 1/4 teaspoon dried oregano
- 2 cups chicken broth
- 1 cup tomato sauce
- Salt and pepper, to taste

For Assembling and Serving:

- 8 large flour tortillas
- Fresh cilantro, chopped (for garnish)
- Sour cream, for serving
- Sliced green onions, for garnish
- Salsa, for serving

Instructions:

Preheat the oven to 375°F (190°C).

In a large mixing bowl, combine the shredded chicken, black beans, corn, diced bell peppers, diced onions, ground cumin, chili powder, salt, and pepper. Mix well.

In a saucepan, heat olive oil over medium heat. Add flour and whisk continuously for 1-2 minutes to make a roux.

Add chili powder, ground cumin, garlic powder, and dried oregano to the roux. Whisk for an additional 1-2 minutes.

Gradually whisk in chicken broth and tomato sauce. Bring the mixture to a simmer, stirring constantly until the sauce thickens.

Season the enchilada sauce with salt and pepper to taste.

Spread a thin layer of enchilada sauce in the bottom of a 9x13-inch baking dish.

Assemble the enchiladas by placing a portion of the chicken filling in the center of each tortilla. Roll the tortilla tightly and place it seam-side down in the baking dish.

Pour the remaining enchilada sauce over the rolled tortillas.

Sprinkle shredded cheese over the top.

Bake in the preheated oven for 20-25 minutes or until the cheese is melted and bubbly.

Remove from the oven and let it rest for a few minutes.

Garnish with chopped cilantro and sliced green onions.

Serve the chicken enchiladas with sour cream and salsa on the side.

Enjoy these delicious and cheesy Chicken Enchiladas!

Turkey Burgers

Ingredients:

- 1 pound (about 450g) ground turkey
- 1/4 cup breadcrumbs
- 1/4 cup finely chopped onion
- 1/4 cup finely chopped bell pepper (any color)
- 2 cloves garlic, minced
- 1 tablespoon Worcestershire sauce
- 1 teaspoon Dijon mustard
- 1 teaspoon dried oregano
- Salt and pepper, to taste
- Olive oil, for cooking
- Burger buns
- Lettuce, tomato, onion, pickles, and other toppings of your choice

Instructions:

In a large bowl, combine ground turkey, breadcrumbs, chopped onion, chopped bell pepper, minced garlic, Worcestershire sauce, Dijon mustard, dried oregano, salt, and pepper. Mix until well combined.
Divide the mixture into equal portions and shape them into burger patties.
Heat olive oil in a skillet or grill pan over medium heat.
Cook the turkey burgers for 5-6 minutes per side or until they are cooked through and reach an internal temperature of 165°F (74°C).
If using a grill, preheat it to medium-high heat and grill the burgers for the same amount of time.
Toast the burger buns in the skillet or on the grill for 1-2 minutes until golden brown.
Assemble the turkey burgers by placing each patty on a bun.
Add lettuce, tomato slices, onion, pickles, or any other toppings of your choice.
Serve the turkey burgers hot and enjoy a lean and flavorful alternative to beef burgers!

Lemon Garlic Roast Chicken

Ingredients:

- 1 whole chicken (about 4-5 pounds)
- 2 lemons, halved
- 1 head of garlic, halved horizontally
- 4 sprigs fresh rosemary
- 4 sprigs fresh thyme
- 2 tablespoons olive oil
- Salt and pepper, to taste
- 1 cup chicken broth (or water)

Instructions:

Preheat the oven to 425°F (220°C).
Rinse the chicken inside and out, and pat it dry with paper towels.
Season the cavity of the chicken with salt and pepper. Stuff the cavity with lemon halves, garlic halves, rosemary, and thyme.
Tie the legs together with kitchen twine and tuck the wings under the body.
Rub the entire chicken with olive oil and season generously with salt and pepper.
Place the chicken in a roasting pan or on a rack in a large baking dish.
Pour chicken broth (or water) into the bottom of the pan to prevent the drippings from burning.
Roast the chicken in the preheated oven for about 1 hour and 15 minutes to 1 hour and 30 minutes, or until the internal temperature reaches 165°F (74°C) and the skin is golden brown and crispy.
Baste the chicken with pan juices every 30 minutes.
Once the chicken is cooked, remove it from the oven and let it rest for 10-15 minutes before carving.
Carve the chicken and serve with the roasted lemons and garlic.
Optionally, use the pan drippings to make a simple gravy by mixing them with a bit of flour or cornstarch over medium heat until thickened.
Enjoy the Lemon Garlic Roast Chicken with your favorite sides!

Teriyaki Salmon

Ingredients:

- 4 salmon fillets
- 1/4 cup soy sauce
- 2 tablespoons mirin (sweet rice wine)
- 2 tablespoons sake (or dry white wine)
- 2 tablespoons brown sugar
- 1 tablespoon honey
- 1 tablespoon sesame oil
- 2 cloves garlic, minced
- 1 teaspoon fresh ginger, grated
- Sesame seeds and chopped green onions (for garnish)
- Cooked white or brown rice (for serving)

Instructions:

In a bowl, whisk together soy sauce, mirin, sake, brown sugar, honey, sesame oil, minced garlic, and grated ginger to make the teriyaki sauce. Set aside.
Pat the salmon fillets dry with paper towels.
Heat a skillet or non-stick pan over medium-high heat.
Place the salmon fillets in the hot skillet, skin-side down, and sear for 2-3 minutes until the skin is crispy and browned.
Flip the salmon fillets and cook for an additional 2-3 minutes on the other side.
Pour the teriyaki sauce over the salmon fillets.
Continue to cook the salmon in the teriyaki sauce, spooning the sauce over the fillets, for 2-3 minutes or until the salmon is cooked through and flakes easily with a fork.
Remove the salmon from the skillet and let it rest for a minute.
Drizzle any remaining teriyaki sauce over the salmon.
Serve the teriyaki salmon over cooked rice.
Garnish with sesame seeds and chopped green onions.
Enjoy this delicious and flavorful Teriyaki Salmon as a quick and satisfying meal!

Chili Con Carne

Ingredients:

- 1 pound (about 450g) ground beef
- 1 large onion, chopped
- 3 cloves garlic, minced
- 1 bell pepper, diced
- 1 jalapeño, seeded and finely chopped (optional, for heat)
- 1 can (14 ounces) diced tomatoes
- 1 can (15 ounces) kidney beans, drained and rinsed
- 1 can (15 ounces) black beans, drained and rinsed
- 1 can (6 ounces) tomato paste
- 2 cups beef broth
- 1 tablespoon chili powder
- 1 teaspoon ground cumin
- 1 teaspoon paprika
- 1/2 teaspoon dried oregano
- 1/2 teaspoon cayenne pepper (adjust to taste, for heat)
- Salt and black pepper, to taste
- Olive oil, for cooking
- Optional toppings: shredded cheddar cheese, sour cream, chopped green onions, cilantro, avocado slices

Instructions:

In a large pot or Dutch oven, heat olive oil over medium heat.
Add chopped onions, minced garlic, and diced bell pepper. Sauté for 5-7 minutes until the vegetables are softened.
Add ground beef to the pot and cook until browned, breaking it up with a spoon as it cooks.
Drain any excess fat from the pot.
Stir in diced tomatoes, kidney beans, black beans, tomato paste, and jalapeño (if using).
Pour in beef broth and mix well.
Add chili powder, ground cumin, paprika, dried oregano, cayenne pepper, salt, and black pepper. Stir to combine.

Bring the chili to a simmer, then reduce the heat to low. Cover and let it simmer for at least 30 minutes to allow the flavors to meld. You can simmer longer for a richer flavor.
Taste and adjust the seasoning if needed.
Serve the chili con carne hot, garnished with your choice of toppings like shredded cheddar cheese, sour cream, chopped green onions, cilantro, and avocado slices.
Enjoy this hearty and flavorful Chili Con Carne!

Chicken Caesar Salad

Ingredients:

For the Caesar Dressing:

- 1/2 cup mayonnaise
- 1/4 cup grated Parmesan cheese
- 2 tablespoons Dijon mustard
- 2 tablespoons lemon juice
- 2 cloves garlic, minced
- 1 teaspoon anchovy paste (optional)
- Salt and black pepper, to taste

For the Salad:

- 2 boneless, skinless chicken breasts
- Salt and black pepper, to taste
- 1 tablespoon olive oil
- 1 head romaine lettuce, washed and chopped
- 1 cup cherry tomatoes, halved
- 1/2 cup croutons
- Additional grated Parmesan cheese (for garnish)

Instructions:

Preheat the oven to 400°F (200°C).
Season the chicken breasts with salt and black pepper on both sides.
Heat olive oil in an oven-safe skillet over medium-high heat.
Sear the chicken breasts for 2-3 minutes per side until browned.
Transfer the skillet to the preheated oven and bake for 20-25 minutes or until the chicken is cooked through and reaches an internal temperature of 165°F (74°C).
While the chicken is baking, prepare the Caesar dressing. In a bowl, whisk together mayonnaise, grated Parmesan cheese, Dijon mustard, lemon juice, minced garlic, anchovy paste (if using), salt, and black pepper. Adjust the seasoning to taste.

Once the chicken is cooked, remove it from the oven and let it rest for a few minutes. Slice the chicken into thin strips.

In a large salad bowl, toss chopped romaine lettuce, cherry tomatoes, and croutons.

Add the sliced chicken on top of the salad.

Drizzle the Caesar dressing over the salad and toss until everything is well coated.

Garnish the salad with additional grated Parmesan cheese.

Serve the Chicken Caesar Salad immediately, and enjoy a classic and satisfying dish!

Pulled Pork Sandwiches

Ingredients:

For the Pulled Pork:

- 3-4 pounds pork shoulder or pork butt
- 2 tablespoons olive oil
- 2 teaspoons smoked paprika
- 2 teaspoons garlic powder
- 2 teaspoons onion powder
- 1 teaspoon cumin
- 1 teaspoon dried oregano
- 1 teaspoon brown sugar
- Salt and black pepper, to taste
- 1 cup chicken or vegetable broth

For the BBQ Sauce:

- 1 cup ketchup
- 1/2 cup apple cider vinegar
- 1/4 cup brown sugar
- 2 tablespoons Dijon mustard
- 2 tablespoons Worcestershire sauce
- 1 tablespoon molasses
- 1 teaspoon smoked paprika
- 1 teaspoon garlic powder
- Salt and black pepper, to taste

For Serving:

- Hamburger buns
- Coleslaw (optional)
- Pickles (optional)

Instructions:

Preheat the oven to 300°F (150°C).
In a small bowl, mix together smoked paprika, garlic powder, onion powder, cumin, dried oregano, brown sugar, salt, and black pepper.
Rub the pork shoulder or pork butt with the spice mixture, ensuring it is well coated.
Heat olive oil in an oven-safe pot or Dutch oven over medium-high heat.
Sear the pork on all sides until browned.
In a separate bowl, mix together the BBQ sauce ingredients: ketchup, apple cider vinegar, brown sugar, Dijon mustard, Worcestershire sauce, molasses, smoked paprika, garlic powder, salt, and black pepper.
Pour the BBQ sauce over the seared pork.
Add chicken or vegetable broth to the pot.
Cover the pot with a lid and transfer it to the preheated oven.
Roast the pork for 3-4 hours or until it is tender and easily pulls apart with a fork.
Once cooked, remove the pork from the oven and shred it using two forks.
Serve the pulled pork on hamburger buns with coleslaw and pickles if desired.
Enjoy these flavorful Pulled Pork Sandwiches as a delicious and comforting meal!

Spicy Chickpea Curry

Ingredients:

- 2 tablespoons vegetable oil
- 1 large onion, finely chopped
- 3 cloves garlic, minced
- 1 tablespoon fresh ginger, grated
- 1 tablespoon curry powder
- 1 teaspoon ground cumin
- 1 teaspoon ground coriander
- 1/2 teaspoon turmeric
- 1/2 teaspoon cayenne pepper (adjust to taste)
- 1 can (15 ounces) chickpeas, drained and rinsed
- 1 can (14 ounces) diced tomatoes
- 1 can (13.5 ounces) coconut milk
- Salt and black pepper, to taste
- Fresh cilantro, chopped (for garnish)
- Cooked rice or naan bread (for serving)

Instructions:

Heat vegetable oil in a large skillet or pan over medium heat.
Add chopped onion to the skillet and sauté until softened and translucent.
Stir in minced garlic and grated ginger, cooking for an additional 1-2 minutes until fragrant.
Add curry powder, ground cumin, ground coriander, turmeric, and cayenne pepper to the skillet. Stir well to coat the onions and garlic with the spices.
Pour in diced tomatoes (with their juices) and chickpeas. Mix to combine.
Pour in coconut milk and stir to create a cohesive curry sauce.
Season the mixture with salt and black pepper to taste.
Bring the curry to a simmer, then reduce the heat to low. Let it simmer for 15-20 minutes to allow the flavors to meld and the chickpeas to absorb the flavors.
Taste and adjust the seasoning if needed.
Serve the spicy chickpea curry over cooked rice or with naan bread.
Garnish with fresh chopped cilantro.
Enjoy this hearty and flavorful Spicy Chickpea Curry as a delicious vegetarian or vegan meal!

Hawaiian Pizza

Ingredients:

- 1 pizza dough (store-bought or homemade)
- 1/2 cup pizza sauce
- 1 1/2 cups shredded mozzarella cheese
- 1 cup cooked ham, diced
- 1/2 cup pineapple chunks, drained
- 1/4 cup red onion, thinly sliced
- 1/4 cup green bell pepper, thinly sliced
- 1/4 cup sliced black olives
- 1/4 cup grated Parmesan cheese
- Crushed red pepper flakes (optional, for added spice)

Instructions:

Preheat the oven to the temperature specified on the pizza dough package or recipe.
Roll out the pizza dough on a floured surface to your desired thickness.
Transfer the rolled-out dough to a pizza stone or baking sheet.
Spread pizza sauce evenly over the dough, leaving a small border around the edges.
Sprinkle shredded mozzarella cheese over the sauce.
Distribute diced ham, pineapple chunks, sliced red onion, sliced green bell pepper, and black olives evenly over the cheese.
Sprinkle grated Parmesan cheese over the toppings.
If desired, add a pinch of crushed red pepper flakes for some heat.
Bake the Hawaiian pizza in the preheated oven according to the pizza dough instructions or until the crust is golden brown and the cheese is melted and bubbly.
Remove the pizza from the oven and let it cool for a few minutes before slicing.
Slice the Hawaiian pizza and serve hot.
Enjoy this delicious and tropical Hawaiian Pizza with the perfect combination of sweet and savory flavors!

Turkey Meatball Soup

Ingredients:

For the Turkey Meatballs:

- 1 pound ground turkey
- 1/2 cup breadcrumbs
- 1/4 cup grated Parmesan cheese
- 1/4 cup chopped fresh parsley
- 1 large egg
- 2 cloves garlic, minced
- 1 teaspoon dried oregano
- Salt and black pepper, to taste

For the Soup:

- 1 tablespoon olive oil
- 1 onion, chopped
- 2 carrots, sliced
- 2 celery stalks, sliced
- 3 cloves garlic, minced
- 8 cups chicken or vegetable broth
- 1 can (14 ounces) diced tomatoes
- 1 cup small pasta (such as orzo or ditalini)
- 1 teaspoon dried thyme
- 1 teaspoon dried rosemary
- Salt and black pepper, to taste
- Fresh parsley, chopped (for garnish)

Instructions:

In a large bowl, mix together ground turkey, breadcrumbs, grated Parmesan cheese, chopped parsley, egg, minced garlic, dried oregano, salt, and black pepper until well combined.
Shape the mixture into small meatballs, about 1 inch in diameter.

In a large pot, heat olive oil over medium heat. Add chopped onion, sliced carrots, sliced celery, and minced garlic. Sauté for 5-7 minutes until the vegetables are softened.

Pour in chicken or vegetable broth and diced tomatoes with their juices. Bring the soup to a simmer.

Add dried thyme and dried rosemary to the pot. Season with salt and black pepper to taste.

Gently drop the turkey meatballs into the simmering soup.

Stir in the small pasta and cook according to the pasta package instructions or until al dente.

Let the soup simmer for an additional 10-15 minutes until the meatballs are cooked through and the flavors meld.

Taste and adjust the seasoning if needed.

Ladle the turkey meatball soup into bowls.

Garnish with chopped fresh parsley.

Serve the delicious and comforting Turkey Meatball Soup hot.

Enjoy this hearty soup as a wholesome and satisfying meal!

Creamy Chicken and Rice Casserole

Ingredients:

- 1 cup long-grain white rice
- 2 cups cooked and shredded chicken (rotisserie chicken works well)
- 1 cup frozen peas
- 1 cup shredded carrots
- 1/2 cup diced celery
- 1/4 cup butter
- 1/4 cup all-purpose flour
- 2 cups chicken broth
- 1 cup milk
- 1 teaspoon dried thyme
- 1/2 teaspoon garlic powder
- Salt and black pepper, to taste
- 1 cup shredded cheddar cheese
- 1/2 cup grated Parmesan cheese
- Fresh parsley, chopped (for garnish)

Instructions:

Preheat the oven to 375°F (190°C).
Cook the rice according to package instructions and set aside.
In a large bowl, combine the cooked and shredded chicken, frozen peas, shredded carrots, and diced celery.
In a saucepan, melt the butter over medium heat.
Stir in the flour to create a roux, and cook for 1-2 minutes until lightly golden.
Gradually whisk in the chicken broth and milk to the roux, ensuring there are no lumps.
Cook the sauce, stirring constantly, until it thickens.
Add dried thyme, garlic powder, salt, and black pepper to the sauce. Adjust the seasoning to taste.
Remove the saucepan from heat and stir in the shredded cheddar cheese and grated Parmesan cheese until melted and smooth.
Combine the cheese sauce with the chicken and vegetable mixture.
Fold in the cooked rice until everything is well coated.
Transfer the mixture to a greased 9x13-inch baking dish.

Bake in the preheated oven for 25-30 minutes or until the casserole is hot and bubbly, and the top is golden brown.

Remove from the oven and let it rest for a few minutes before serving.

Garnish the Creamy Chicken and Rice Casserole with chopped fresh parsley.

Serve this comforting casserole as a delicious and satisfying meal!

Caprese Chicken

Ingredients:

- 4 boneless, skinless chicken breasts
- Salt and black pepper, to taste
- 2 tablespoons olive oil
- 4 slices fresh mozzarella cheese
- 4 slices ripe tomato
- Fresh basil leaves
- Balsamic glaze, for drizzling (optional)

Instructions:

Preheat the oven to 400°F (200°C).
Season the chicken breasts with salt and black pepper on both sides.
Heat olive oil in an oven-safe skillet over medium-high heat.
Add the chicken breasts to the skillet and sear for 2-3 minutes on each side until golden brown.
Place a slice of fresh mozzarella cheese on top of each chicken breast.
Top the mozzarella with a slice of ripe tomato.
Transfer the skillet to the preheated oven and bake for 15-20 minutes or until the chicken is cooked through and the cheese is melted and bubbly.
Remove the skillet from the oven.
Garnish each chicken breast with fresh basil leaves.
Drizzle balsamic glaze over the top if desired.
Serve the Caprese Chicken hot, and enjoy this flavorful and elegant dish!

Tofu Stir-Fry

Ingredients:

For the Stir-Fry Sauce:

- 1/4 cup soy sauce
- 2 tablespoons hoisin sauce
- 1 tablespoon rice vinegar
- 1 tablespoon sesame oil
- 1 tablespoon maple syrup or agave nectar
- 1 teaspoon cornstarch

For the Tofu:

- 1 block (14-16 ounces) extra-firm tofu, pressed and cubed
- 2 tablespoons soy sauce
- 1 tablespoon sesame oil

For the Stir-Fry:

- 2 tablespoons vegetable oil
- 1 bell pepper, thinly sliced
- 1 carrot, julienned
- 1 cup broccoli florets
- 1 cup snap peas, trimmed
- 2 cloves garlic, minced
- 1 tablespoon fresh ginger, grated
- Cooked rice or noodles (for serving)
- Sesame seeds and chopped green onions (for garnish)

Instructions:

In a small bowl, whisk together the ingredients for the stir-fry sauce: soy sauce, hoisin sauce, rice vinegar, sesame oil, maple syrup or agave nectar, and cornstarch. Set aside.

Press the tofu to remove excess water, then cut it into cubes. Marinate the tofu cubes in soy sauce and sesame oil for about 15 minutes.

Heat vegetable oil in a large skillet or wok over medium-high heat.

Add the marinated tofu cubes to the skillet and stir-fry until they are golden brown on all sides. Remove the tofu from the skillet and set aside.

In the same skillet, add a bit more oil if needed. Sauté bell pepper, julienned carrot, broccoli florets, and snap peas until they are crisp-tender.

Add minced garlic and grated ginger to the vegetables, and stir-fry for another minute until fragrant.

Return the cooked tofu to the skillet.

Pour the prepared stir-fry sauce over the tofu and vegetables. Toss everything together until well coated and heated through.

Serve the tofu stir-fry over cooked rice or noodles.

Garnish with sesame seeds and chopped green onions.

Enjoy this flavorful and healthy Tofu Stir-Fry as a delicious meatless meal!

Baked Chicken Nuggets

Ingredients:

- 1 pound boneless, skinless chicken breasts, cut into bite-sized pieces
- 1 cup breadcrumbs
- 1/2 cup grated Parmesan cheese
- 1 teaspoon garlic powder
- 1 teaspoon onion powder
- 1/2 teaspoon paprika
- 1/2 teaspoon salt
- 1/4 teaspoon black pepper
- 2 large eggs, beaten
- Cooking spray or olive oil

Instructions:

Preheat the oven to 400°F (200°C). Line a baking sheet with parchment paper and lightly coat it with cooking spray or olive oil.
In a shallow bowl, combine breadcrumbs, grated Parmesan cheese, garlic powder, onion powder, paprika, salt, and black pepper. Mix well.
Dip each piece of chicken into the beaten eggs, allowing any excess to drip off.
Roll the chicken pieces in the breadcrumb mixture, ensuring they are well coated on all sides. Press the breadcrumbs onto the chicken for better adherence.
Place the coated chicken nuggets on the prepared baking sheet, leaving some space between each piece.
Lightly spray the tops of the chicken nuggets with cooking spray or drizzle with a little olive oil.
Bake in the preheated oven for 15-18 minutes or until the chicken is cooked through and the nuggets are golden brown.
If desired, flip the nuggets halfway through the baking time for even browning.
Remove the baked chicken nuggets from the oven and let them rest for a few minutes before serving.
Serve the chicken nuggets with your favorite dipping sauce, such as ketchup, barbecue sauce, or honey mustard.
Enjoy these homemade Baked Chicken Nuggets as a healthier alternative to the classic fried version!

Vegetable Pizza

Ingredients:

For the Pizza Dough:

- 1 package (about 2 1/4 teaspoons) active dry yeast
- 1 teaspoon sugar
- 3/4 cup warm water (110°F/43°C)
- 2 cups all-purpose flour
- 1 teaspoon salt
- 1 tablespoon olive oil

For the Pizza Sauce:

- 1 cup tomato sauce
- 1 teaspoon dried oregano
- 1 teaspoon dried basil
- 1/2 teaspoon garlic powder
- Salt and black pepper, to taste

For the Toppings:

- 1 cup shredded mozzarella cheese
- 1/2 cup cherry tomatoes, sliced in half
- 1/2 cup bell peppers, thinly sliced
- 1/2 cup red onion, thinly sliced
- 1/2 cup black olives, sliced
- Fresh basil leaves, for garnish

Instructions:

Preheat the oven to 475°F (245°C). If you have a pizza stone, place it in the oven during preheating.

In a small bowl, combine active dry yeast, sugar, and warm water. Let it sit for about 5 minutes until foamy.

In a large mixing bowl, combine all-purpose flour and salt. Make a well in the center.
Pour the yeast mixture and olive oil into the well. Stir until the dough comes together.
Turn the dough out onto a floured surface and knead for about 5 minutes until smooth.
Place the dough in a greased bowl, cover with a kitchen towel, and let it rise in a warm place for 1-2 hours or until doubled in size.
While the dough is rising, prepare the pizza sauce by combining tomato sauce, dried oregano, dried basil, garlic powder, salt, and black pepper in a bowl. Mix well and set aside.
Once the dough has risen, punch it down and roll it out on a floured surface to your desired thickness.
If using a pizza stone, transfer the rolled-out dough onto a piece of parchment paper.
Spread the pizza sauce over the dough, leaving a small border around the edges.
Sprinkle shredded mozzarella cheese over the sauce.
Arrange sliced cherry tomatoes, bell peppers, red onion, and black olives on top of the cheese.
If using a pizza stone, carefully transfer the parchment paper with the pizza onto the preheated stone in the oven.
Bake in the preheated oven for 12-15 minutes or until the crust is golden and the cheese is melted and bubbly.
If not using a pizza stone, simply place the prepared pizza on a baking sheet and bake.
Remove the vegetable pizza from the oven and let it cool for a few minutes.
Garnish with fresh basil leaves.
Slice and serve the delicious Vegetable Pizza hot.
Enjoy this homemade pizza with a variety of colorful and flavorful vegetable toppings!

Chicken and Broccoli Alfredo

Ingredients:

- 8 ounces fettuccine pasta
- 2 tablespoons unsalted butter
- 1 pound boneless, skinless chicken breasts, cut into bite-sized pieces
- Salt and black pepper, to taste
- 2 cloves garlic, minced
- 1 cup broccoli florets
- 1 cup heavy cream
- 1 cup grated Parmesan cheese
- 1/2 teaspoon garlic powder
- 1/2 teaspoon onion powder
- 1/4 teaspoon nutmeg (optional)
- Fresh parsley, chopped (for garnish)

Instructions:

Cook the fettuccine pasta according to package instructions. Drain and set aside.
In a large skillet, melt the butter over medium-high heat.
Season the chicken pieces with salt and black pepper.
Add the seasoned chicken to the skillet and cook until browned on all sides and cooked through. Remove the chicken from the skillet and set aside.
In the same skillet, add minced garlic and broccoli florets. Sauté until the broccoli is tender-crisp.
Pour in the heavy cream and bring it to a simmer.
Stir in grated Parmesan cheese, garlic powder, onion powder, and nutmeg (if using). Continue stirring until the cheese is melted and the sauce is smooth.
Return the cooked chicken to the skillet and stir to coat it with the Alfredo sauce.
Add the cooked fettuccine pasta to the skillet and toss until everything is well coated in the creamy sauce.
Adjust the seasoning with salt and black pepper if needed.
Serve the Chicken and Broccoli Alfredo hot, garnished with chopped fresh parsley.
Enjoy this comforting and indulgent pasta dish as a delicious meal!

Sweet Potato Black Bean Quesadillas

Ingredients:

- 2 large sweet potatoes, peeled and diced
- 1 can (15 ounces) black beans, drained and rinsed
- 1 teaspoon ground cumin
- 1 teaspoon chili powder
- 1/2 teaspoon smoked paprika
- Salt and black pepper, to taste
- 1 tablespoon olive oil
- 4 large whole wheat or corn tortillas
- 1 1/2 cups shredded cheese (cheddar, Monterey Jack, or a blend)
- 1 avocado, sliced
- Fresh cilantro, chopped (for garnish)
- Lime wedges (for serving)

Instructions:

Preheat the oven to 400°F (200°C).
In a bowl, toss the diced sweet potatoes with cumin, chili powder, smoked paprika, salt, black pepper, and olive oil until well coated.
Spread the seasoned sweet potatoes on a baking sheet in a single layer.
Roast in the preheated oven for 20-25 minutes or until the sweet potatoes are tender and lightly browned, stirring halfway through.
In a large bowl, mash the black beans with a fork or potato masher.
Once the sweet potatoes are roasted, add them to the mashed black beans and mix well.
Heat a large skillet over medium heat.
Place a tortilla in the skillet and spread a portion of the sweet potato and black bean mixture over half of the tortilla.
Sprinkle shredded cheese over the sweet potato and black bean mixture.
Fold the tortilla in half, creating a quesadilla.
Cook the quesadilla in the skillet for 2-3 minutes on each side or until the tortilla is golden brown and the cheese is melted.
Repeat the process for the remaining tortillas and filling.
Once cooked, slice the quesadillas into wedges.
Serve the Sweet Potato Black Bean Quesadillas with sliced avocado, chopped cilantro, and lime wedges.

Enjoy these flavorful and nutritious quesadillas as a delicious and satisfying meal!

One-Pan Baked Zucchini and Tomato Chicken

Ingredients:

- 4 boneless, skinless chicken breasts
- Salt and black pepper, to taste
- 2 tablespoons olive oil
- 3 cloves garlic, minced
- 1 teaspoon dried oregano
- 1 teaspoon dried basil
- 1/2 teaspoon dried thyme
- 1/2 teaspoon dried rosemary
- 2 medium zucchinis, sliced
- 1 cup cherry tomatoes, halved
- 1/4 cup grated Parmesan cheese (optional)
- Fresh basil leaves, chopped (for garnish)

Instructions:

Preheat the oven to 400°F (200°C).
Season the chicken breasts with salt and black pepper on both sides.
Heat olive oil in an oven-safe skillet over medium-high heat.
Add the seasoned chicken breasts to the skillet and sear for 2-3 minutes on each side until golden brown.
In a small bowl, mix together minced garlic, dried oregano, dried basil, dried thyme, and dried rosemary.
Sprinkle half of the herb mixture over the seared chicken breasts.
Arrange sliced zucchinis and halved cherry tomatoes around the chicken in the skillet.
Sprinkle the remaining herb mixture over the vegetables.
If desired, sprinkle grated Parmesan cheese over the chicken and vegetables.
Transfer the skillet to the preheated oven and bake for 20-25 minutes or until the chicken is cooked through and the vegetables are tender.
Once cooked, remove the skillet from the oven.
Garnish with chopped fresh basil leaves.
Serve the One-Pan Baked Zucchini and Tomato Chicken hot.
Enjoy this easy and delicious one-pan meal with a burst of flavors!

Creamy Tomato Basil Pasta

Ingredients:

- 8 ounces (about 225g) penne or your favorite pasta
- 2 tablespoons olive oil
- 3 cloves garlic, minced
- 1 can (28 ounces) crushed tomatoes
- 1/2 cup heavy cream
- 1 teaspoon dried basil
- Salt and black pepper, to taste
- 1/4 teaspoon red pepper flakes (optional, for some heat)
- 1/2 cup grated Parmesan cheese
- Fresh basil leaves, chopped (for garnish)

Instructions:

Cook the pasta according to package instructions. Drain and set aside.
In a large skillet, heat olive oil over medium heat.
Add minced garlic to the skillet and sauté for 1-2 minutes until fragrant.
Pour in the crushed tomatoes and bring the mixture to a simmer.
Stir in heavy cream, dried basil, salt, black pepper, and red pepper flakes (if using). Mix well.
Simmer the tomato cream sauce for 5-7 minutes, allowing the flavors to meld.
Stir in grated Parmesan cheese until melted and the sauce is creamy.
Add the cooked pasta to the skillet and toss until the pasta is well coated in the creamy tomato basil sauce.
Taste and adjust the seasoning if needed.
Garnish with chopped fresh basil leaves.
Serve the Creamy Tomato Basil Pasta hot.
Enjoy this simple and flavorful pasta dish as a comforting and satisfying meal!

Buffalo Chicken Wraps

Ingredients:

For the Buffalo Chicken:

- 1 pound boneless, skinless chicken breasts, cooked and shredded
- 1/2 cup buffalo sauce
- 2 tablespoons unsalted butter, melted
- 1 tablespoon white vinegar
- 1/2 teaspoon garlic powder
- Salt and black pepper, to taste

For the Wraps:

- 4 large flour tortillas
- 1 cup shredded lettuce
- 1 cup diced tomatoes
- 1/2 cup crumbled blue cheese or ranch dressing
- 1/4 cup chopped green onions
- 1/4 cup chopped celery (optional)
- Ranch or blue cheese dressing (for drizzling, optional)

Instructions:

In a bowl, combine the shredded chicken with buffalo sauce, melted butter, white vinegar, garlic powder, salt, and black pepper. Mix well until the chicken is evenly coated.
Heat a skillet over medium heat and warm the flour tortillas for about 15-20 seconds on each side.
Lay out the warmed tortillas on a flat surface.
Distribute the shredded lettuce, diced tomatoes, buffalo chicken, crumbled blue cheese or ranch dressing, chopped green onions, and chopped celery (if using) evenly among the tortillas.
Drizzle with additional ranch or blue cheese dressing if desired.
Fold the sides of each tortilla in, then roll them up tightly to form wraps.
Serve the Buffalo Chicken Wraps immediately.

Enjoy these flavorful and spicy wraps as a delicious meal or snack!

Lemon Herb Grilled Chicken

Ingredients:

- 4 boneless, skinless chicken breasts
- Zest and juice of 2 lemons
- 3 tablespoons olive oil
- 2 cloves garlic, minced
- 1 teaspoon dried thyme
- 1 teaspoon dried rosemary
- 1 teaspoon dried oregano
- Salt and black pepper, to taste
- Fresh parsley, chopped (for garnish)

Instructions:

In a bowl, whisk together the lemon zest, lemon juice, olive oil, minced garlic, dried thyme, dried rosemary, dried oregano, salt, and black pepper.
Place the chicken breasts in a resealable plastic bag or shallow dish.
Pour the marinade over the chicken, ensuring it's well coated. Seal the bag or cover the dish and refrigerate for at least 30 minutes, or preferably up to 4 hours.
Preheat the grill to medium-high heat.
Remove the chicken from the marinade, allowing any excess to drip off.
Grill the chicken for about 6-8 minutes per side or until fully cooked, with an internal temperature of 165°F (74°C).
Baste the chicken with any remaining marinade during grilling.
Once cooked, remove the chicken from the grill and let it rest for a few minutes.
Garnish the Lemon Herb Grilled Chicken with chopped fresh parsley.
Serve hot and enjoy this flavorful and zesty grilled chicken as a delicious main dish!

Teriyaki Veggie Bowl

Ingredients:

For the Teriyaki Sauce:

- 1/2 cup soy sauce
- 1/4 cup water
- 2 tablespoons rice vinegar
- 2 tablespoons brown sugar
- 1 tablespoon honey
- 2 teaspoons minced garlic
- 1 teaspoon minced ginger
- 1 tablespoon cornstarch (mixed with 2 tablespoons water to create a slurry)

For the Veggie Bowl:

- 2 cups broccoli florets
- 1 bell pepper, sliced
- 1 carrot, julienned
- 1 zucchini, sliced
- 1 cup snap peas, trimmed
- 1 cup sliced mushrooms
- 1 tablespoon vegetable oil
- Cooked rice or quinoa (for serving)
- Sesame seeds and chopped green onions (for garnish)

Instructions:

In a small saucepan, combine soy sauce, water, rice vinegar, brown sugar, honey, minced garlic, and minced ginger. Heat over medium heat until the mixture comes to a simmer.
In a separate small bowl, mix the cornstarch with 2 tablespoons of water to create a slurry.
Gradually whisk the cornstarch slurry into the simmering sauce, stirring constantly. Continue to cook until the sauce thickens. Remove from heat and set aside.
In a large skillet or wok, heat vegetable oil over medium-high heat.

Add broccoli, bell pepper, carrot, zucchini, snap peas, and mushrooms to the skillet. Stir-fry the vegetables for 5-7 minutes or until they are crisp-tender.
Pour the prepared teriyaki sauce over the vegetables and toss to coat evenly. Continue cooking for an additional 2-3 minutes until the vegetables are coated and heated through.
Serve the Teriyaki Veggie Bowl over cooked rice or quinoa.
Garnish with sesame seeds and chopped green onions.
Enjoy this delicious and colorful Teriyaki Veggie Bowl as a wholesome and flavorful meal!

Chicken and Rice Burrito Bowls

Ingredients:

For the Chicken Marinade:

- 1 pound boneless, skinless chicken breasts, cut into bite-sized pieces
- 2 tablespoons olive oil
- 1 teaspoon ground cumin
- 1 teaspoon chili powder
- 1 teaspoon smoked paprika
- 1 teaspoon garlic powder
- Salt and black pepper, to taste
- Juice of 1 lime

For the Burrito Bowls:

- 1 cup white or brown rice, cooked
- 1 can (15 ounces) black beans, drained and rinsed
- 1 cup corn kernels (fresh, frozen, or canned)
- 1 cup cherry tomatoes, halved
- 1 avocado, sliced
- 1/2 cup shredded cheese (cheddar, Monterey Jack, or a blend)
- Fresh cilantro, chopped (for garnish)
- Lime wedges (for serving)

Optional Toppings:

- Sour cream
- Salsa
- Hot sauce

Instructions:

In a bowl, combine the olive oil, ground cumin, chili powder, smoked paprika, garlic powder, salt, black pepper, and lime juice to create the chicken marinade.

Add the bite-sized chicken pieces to the marinade, ensuring they are well coated. Let it marinate for at least 30 minutes, or preferably up to 4 hours.

Heat a skillet over medium-high heat. Cook the marinated chicken until fully cooked and browned on all sides. Set aside.

In each serving bowl, assemble the burrito bowls by dividing the cooked rice, black beans, corn kernels, cherry tomatoes, avocado slices, and shredded cheese among the bowls.

Top each bowl with the cooked and seasoned chicken.

Garnish with chopped fresh cilantro and serve with lime wedges on the side.

Optionally, add toppings like sour cream, salsa, or hot sauce to taste.

Enjoy these Chicken and Rice Burrito Bowls as a customizable and flavorful meal!

Beef and Mushroom Stroganoff

Ingredients:

- 1 pound (450g) beef sirloin or tenderloin, thinly sliced
- Salt and black pepper, to taste
- 2 tablespoons olive oil
- 1 onion, finely chopped
- 2 cloves garlic, minced
- 8 ounces (225g) mushrooms, sliced
- 2 tablespoons all-purpose flour
- 1 cup beef broth
- 1 tablespoon Worcestershire sauce
- 1 teaspoon Dijon mustard
- 1/2 cup sour cream
- 1 tablespoon chopped fresh parsley (for garnish)
- Cooked egg noodles or rice (for serving)

Instructions:

Season the sliced beef with salt and black pepper.
In a large skillet, heat olive oil over medium-high heat.
Add the sliced beef to the skillet and cook until browned on all sides. Remove the beef from the skillet and set aside.
In the same skillet, add chopped onion and cook until softened.
Add minced garlic and sliced mushrooms to the skillet. Cook until the mushrooms are golden brown and most of their liquid has evaporated.
Sprinkle flour over the mushroom mixture and stir well to coat.
Pour in the beef broth, Worcestershire sauce, and Dijon mustard. Stir to combine and bring the mixture to a simmer.
Return the cooked beef to the skillet and let it simmer in the sauce for a few minutes until the beef is heated through and the sauce thickens.
Reduce the heat to low and stir in the sour cream. Heat the stroganoff gently, but do not let it boil.
Season with additional salt and black pepper, if needed.
Serve the Beef and Mushroom Stroganoff over cooked egg noodles or rice.
Garnish with chopped fresh parsley.

Enjoy this classic and comforting Beef and Mushroom Stroganoff as a delicious and hearty meal!

Pesto Pasta with Cherry Tomatoes

Ingredients:

- 8 ounces (about 225g) penne or your favorite pasta
- 2 cups cherry tomatoes, halved
- 1/2 cup fresh basil leaves
- 1/3 cup pine nuts
- 1/2 cup grated Parmesan cheese
- 2 cloves garlic, minced
- 1/2 cup extra-virgin olive oil
- Salt and black pepper, to taste
- Red pepper flakes (optional, for some heat)
- Additional grated Parmesan (for serving)

Instructions:

Cook the pasta according to package instructions. Drain and set aside.
In a food processor, combine cherry tomatoes, fresh basil leaves, pine nuts, grated Parmesan cheese, and minced garlic.
Pulse the ingredients until well combined.
With the food processor running, slowly stream in the extra-virgin olive oil until the pesto reaches a smooth consistency.
Season the pesto with salt and black pepper to taste. Add red pepper flakes if you want some heat.
In a large mixing bowl, toss the cooked pasta with the prepared pesto until the pasta is evenly coated.
Serve the Pesto Pasta with Cherry Tomatoes hot or at room temperature.
Garnish with additional grated Parmesan.
Enjoy this flavorful and vibrant Pesto Pasta with Cherry Tomatoes as a delicious and easy-to-make meal!

Veggie-loaded Spaghetti Carbonara

Ingredients:

- 8 ounces (about 225g) spaghetti
- 1 tablespoon olive oil
- 1 onion, finely chopped
- 2 cloves garlic, minced
- 1 cup mushrooms, sliced
- 1 zucchini, diced
- 1 red bell pepper, diced
- 1 cup frozen peas, thawed
- 2 large eggs
- 1 cup grated Pecorino Romano cheese
- Salt and black pepper, to taste
- Fresh parsley, chopped (for garnish)

Instructions:

Cook the spaghetti according to package instructions. Drain and set aside.
In a large skillet, heat olive oil over medium heat.
Add chopped onion and sauté until softened.
Add minced garlic, sliced mushrooms, diced zucchini, and diced red bell pepper to the skillet. Sauté until the vegetables are tender.
Stir in the thawed peas and cook for an additional 1-2 minutes.
In a bowl, whisk together the eggs and grated Pecorino Romano cheese until well combined.
Pour the egg and cheese mixture over the cooked and drained spaghetti. Toss quickly to coat the pasta.
Add the sautéed vegetables to the spaghetti and toss until the vegetables are evenly distributed.
Season with salt and black pepper to taste.
Garnish with chopped fresh parsley.
Serve the Veggie-loaded Spaghetti Carbonara hot.
Enjoy this delicious and veggie-packed twist on traditional spaghetti carbonara!

Oven-Baked BBQ Chicken

Ingredients:

- 4 bone-in, skin-on chicken thighs
- Salt and black pepper, to taste
- 1 cup barbecue sauce
- 2 tablespoons olive oil
- 1 teaspoon smoked paprika
- 1 teaspoon garlic powder
- 1 teaspoon onion powder
- 1/2 teaspoon dried thyme
- 1/2 teaspoon dried oregano
- 1/2 teaspoon dried rosemary

Instructions:

Preheat the oven to 400°F (200°C).
Season the chicken thighs with salt and black pepper on both sides.
In a bowl, whisk together barbecue sauce, olive oil, smoked paprika, garlic powder, onion powder, dried thyme, dried oregano, and dried rosemary.
Place the chicken thighs in a large resealable plastic bag or a shallow dish.
Pour half of the barbecue sauce mixture over the chicken thighs, making sure they are well coated. Reserve the remaining sauce for basting.
Marinate the chicken in the refrigerator for at least 30 minutes, or preferably up to 4 hours.
Place the marinated chicken thighs on a baking sheet lined with parchment paper or aluminum foil.
Bake in the preheated oven for 30-40 minutes or until the chicken reaches an internal temperature of 165°F (74°C), basting with the reserved barbecue sauce every 15 minutes.
If desired, broil the chicken for an additional 2-3 minutes at the end to crisp up the skin.
Remove the oven-baked BBQ chicken from the oven and let it rest for a few minutes before serving.
Serve the chicken hot with your favorite sides.
Enjoy this easy and flavorful Oven-Baked BBQ Chicken for a delicious meal!

Lemon Garlic Shrimp Pasta

Ingredients:

- 8 ounces (about 225g) linguine or your favorite pasta
- 1 pound (about 450g) large shrimp, peeled and deveined
- Salt and black pepper, to taste
- 3 tablespoons olive oil
- 4 cloves garlic, minced
- Zest of 1 lemon
- Juice of 1 lemon
- 1/2 teaspoon red pepper flakes (optional, for some heat)
- 1/2 cup cherry tomatoes, halved
- 1/4 cup chopped fresh parsley
- Grated Parmesan cheese (for serving)

Instructions:

Cook the pasta according to package instructions. Drain and set aside.
Season the shrimp with salt and black pepper.
In a large skillet, heat olive oil over medium-high heat.
Add the seasoned shrimp to the skillet and cook for 2-3 minutes per side or until they are pink and opaque. Remove the shrimp from the skillet and set aside.
In the same skillet, add minced garlic and sauté for about 1 minute until fragrant.
Add lemon zest, lemon juice, and red pepper flakes (if using) to the skillet. Stir to combine.
Toss in the halved cherry tomatoes and cook for an additional 2 minutes until they start to soften.
Return the cooked shrimp to the skillet and toss to coat in the lemon garlic sauce. Cook for an additional 1-2 minutes to heat the shrimp through.
Add the cooked pasta to the skillet and toss until everything is well coated.
Season with additional salt and black pepper if needed.
Garnish with chopped fresh parsley.
Serve the Lemon Garlic Shrimp Pasta hot, topped with grated Parmesan cheese.
Enjoy this quick and flavorful shrimp pasta as a delightful and satisfying meal!

Broccoli Cheddar Stuffed Potatoes

Ingredients:

- 4 large baking potatoes
- 2 tablespoons olive oil
- Salt and black pepper, to taste
- 2 cups broccoli florets, steamed or boiled
- 1 1/2 cups shredded cheddar cheese
- 1/2 cup sour cream
- 1/4 cup chopped green onions
- 1/4 cup chopped fresh parsley (optional, for garnish)

Instructions:

Preheat the oven to 400°F (200°C).
Scrub the potatoes thoroughly and pat them dry. Prick each potato several times with a fork.
Rub each potato with olive oil and sprinkle with salt and black pepper.
Place the potatoes directly on the oven rack and bake for 45-60 minutes or until the potatoes are tender when pierced with a fork.
While the potatoes are baking, steam or boil the broccoli florets until they are tender-crisp. Drain and set aside.
Once the potatoes are done, remove them from the oven and let them cool slightly.
Slice off the top third of each potato and scoop out the flesh, leaving a thin layer inside the skins.
In a bowl, mash the scooped-out potato flesh. Mix in the steamed broccoli, shredded cheddar cheese, sour cream, and chopped green onions.
Stuff each potato skin with the broccoli cheddar mixture.
Place the stuffed potatoes back in the oven for an additional 10-15 minutes, or until the cheese is melted and bubbly.
Remove from the oven and garnish with chopped fresh parsley if desired.
Serve the Broccoli Cheddar Stuffed Potatoes hot.
Enjoy these delicious and cheesy stuffed potatoes as a comforting and satisfying meal!

Turkey and Veggie Skillet

Ingredients:

- 1 pound ground turkey
- 1 tablespoon olive oil
- 1 onion, finely chopped
- 2 cloves garlic, minced
- 1 bell pepper, diced
- 1 zucchini, diced
- 1 cup cherry tomatoes, halved
- 1 cup corn kernels (fresh, frozen, or canned)
- 1 teaspoon ground cumin
- 1 teaspoon chili powder
- 1/2 teaspoon paprika
- Salt and black pepper, to taste
- 1 cup cooked quinoa or rice
- Fresh cilantro, chopped (for garnish)
- Lime wedges (for serving)

Instructions:

In a large skillet, heat olive oil over medium-high heat.
Add ground turkey to the skillet and cook until browned, breaking it apart with a spoon as it cooks.
Add chopped onion and minced garlic to the skillet. Sauté until the onion is softened.
Stir in diced bell pepper, diced zucchini, cherry tomatoes, and corn kernels. Cook for an additional 5-7 minutes until the vegetables are tender.
Season the mixture with ground cumin, chili powder, paprika, salt, and black pepper. Mix well.
Add cooked quinoa or rice to the skillet and stir to combine.
Cook for an additional 2-3 minutes until everything is heated through.
Taste and adjust the seasoning if needed.
Garnish with chopped fresh cilantro.
Serve the Turkey and Veggie Skillet hot, with lime wedges on the side.
Enjoy this quick and nutritious turkey and veggie dish as a delicious and well-balanced meal!

Chicken Fajita Bowls

Ingredients:

For the Chicken Marinade:

- 1 pound boneless, skinless chicken breasts, sliced
- 2 tablespoons olive oil
- 1 teaspoon ground cumin
- 1 teaspoon chili powder
- 1 teaspoon paprika
- 1 teaspoon garlic powder
- Salt and black pepper, to taste
- Juice of 1 lime

For the Fajita Bowls:

- 2 tablespoons olive oil
- 1 onion, sliced
- 1 bell pepper, sliced (any color)
- 1 zucchini, sliced
- 1 cup cherry tomatoes, halved
- Cooked rice or quinoa (for serving)
- Fresh cilantro, chopped (for garnish)
- Lime wedges (for serving)
- Salsa, sour cream, or guacamole (optional, for topping)

Instructions:

> In a bowl, combine the olive oil, ground cumin, chili powder, paprika, garlic powder, salt, black pepper, and lime juice to create the chicken marinade.
> Add the sliced chicken breasts to the marinade, ensuring they are well coated. Let it marinate for at least 30 minutes, or preferably up to 4 hours.
> Heat a large skillet over medium-high heat. Add 2 tablespoons of olive oil.
> Add sliced onion, bell pepper, and zucchini to the skillet. Cook for 5-7 minutes until the vegetables are tender-crisp.
> Push the vegetables to one side of the skillet and add the marinated chicken to the other side. Cook the chicken until browned and cooked through.
> Once the chicken is cooked, mix it with the sautéed vegetables in the skillet.

Add cherry tomatoes and cook for an additional 2 minutes until they are slightly softened.

Serve the Chicken Fajita Bowls over cooked rice or quinoa.

Garnish with chopped fresh cilantro and lime wedges.

Optionally, top with salsa, sour cream, or guacamole.

Enjoy these flavorful and colorful Chicken Fajita Bowls as a delicious and satisfying meal!

Spinach and Feta Stuffed Chicken Breast

Ingredients:

- 4 boneless, skinless chicken breasts
- Salt and black pepper, to taste
- 1 tablespoon olive oil
- 2 cups fresh spinach, chopped
- 1/2 cup crumbled feta cheese
- 2 cloves garlic, minced
- 1 teaspoon dried oregano
- 1 teaspoon dried thyme
- 1 teaspoon dried basil
- 1/2 teaspoon onion powder
- Toothpicks or kitchen twine (for securing)

Instructions:

Preheat the oven to 375°F (190°C).
Season the chicken breasts with salt and black pepper.
In a skillet, heat olive oil over medium heat.
Add chopped spinach to the skillet and cook until wilted.
Stir in crumbled feta cheese, minced garlic, dried oregano, dried thyme, dried basil, and onion powder. Cook for an additional 2 minutes until the mixture is well combined.
Make a horizontal cut into the thickest part of each chicken breast to create a pocket for stuffing. Be careful not to cut all the way through.
Stuff each chicken breast with the spinach and feta mixture.
Secure the stuffed chicken breasts with toothpicks or tie them with kitchen twine to keep the filling in place.
Season the outside of the chicken breasts with additional salt and black pepper.
Heat a large oven-safe skillet over medium-high heat.
Add the stuffed chicken breasts to the skillet and sear for 2-3 minutes on each side until golden brown.
Transfer the skillet to the preheated oven and bake for 20-25 minutes or until the chicken is cooked through.
Once cooked, remove the skillet from the oven.

Let the Spinach and Feta Stuffed Chicken Breast rest for a few minutes before serving.

Remove toothpicks or kitchen twine before serving.

Enjoy this flavorful and elegant stuffed chicken dish as a delicious and wholesome meal!

Mediterranean Quinoa Salad

Ingredients:

- 1 cup quinoa, rinsed and cooked according to package instructions
- 2 cups cherry tomatoes, halved
- 1 cucumber, diced
- 1 red bell pepper, diced
- 1/2 red onion, finely chopped
- 1/2 cup Kalamata olives, pitted and sliced
- 1/2 cup crumbled feta cheese
- 1/4 cup fresh parsley, chopped
- 1/4 cup fresh mint, chopped (optional)
- 1/4 cup extra-virgin olive oil
- 2 tablespoons red wine vinegar
- 1 clove garlic, minced
- 1 teaspoon dried oregano
- Salt and black pepper, to taste
- Lemon wedges (for serving)

Instructions:

In a large bowl, combine the cooked quinoa, cherry tomatoes, cucumber, red bell pepper, red onion, Kalamata olives, feta cheese, fresh parsley, and fresh mint.

In a small bowl or jar, whisk together the extra-virgin olive oil, red wine vinegar, minced garlic, dried oregano, salt, and black pepper to create the dressing.

Pour the dressing over the quinoa and vegetable mixture. Toss everything together until well combined.

Taste and adjust the seasoning if needed.

Refrigerate the Mediterranean Quinoa Salad for at least 30 minutes to allow the flavors to meld.

Before serving, give the salad a final toss and garnish with additional fresh herbs if desired.

Serve the salad chilled, accompanied by lemon wedges.

Enjoy this refreshing and nutritious Mediterranean Quinoa Salad as a side dish or a light and satisfying main meal!

www.ingramcontent.com/pod-product-compliance
Lightning Source LLC
LaVergne TN
LVHW081617060526
838201LV00054B/2282